Making Sense *of the* COMMON CORE

How To Incorporate Math and ELA in Your K-5 Music Classroom

BY SHARON BURCH

DIGITAL DOWNLOAD CODE
To access digital files of the CCSS charts & templates in Appendixes A, B & C, go to:
www.halleonard.com/mylibrary

Enter Code
4630-0628-1292-8

T0039747

Shawnee Press

EXCLUSIVELY DISTRIBUTED BY

HAL•LEONARD®
CORPORATION
7777 W. BLUEMOUND RD. P.O. BOX 13819 MILWAUKEE, WI 53213

Visit Hal Leonard Online at
www.halleonard.com
Visit Shawnee Press Online at
www.shawneepress.com

ISBN-13: 978-1-49500-838-2

Published by Hal Leonard Corporation
7777 W. Bluemound Road
P.O. Box 13819
Milwaukee, WI 53213

Library of Congress Cataloging-in-Publication Data

Burch, Sharon (Sharon Kay).
  Making sense of the Common Core : incorporating math and ELA in your K-5 music classroom / by Sharon Burch. -- First edition.
      pages cm
1. Music--Instruction and study--United States. 2. Language arts (Kindergarten)--Standards--United States. 3. Language arts (Elementary)--Standards--United States. 4. Mathematics--Study and teaching (Kindergarten)--Standards--United States. 5. Mathematics--Study and teaching (Elementary)--Standards--United States. I. Title.
  MT3.U5B87 2015
  372.87›043--dc23
                              2014041168

Printed in the U.S.A.
First Edition

Visit Hal Leonard Online at **www.halleonard.com**

Visit Hal Leonard Online at www.halleonard.com
Visit Shawnee Press Online at www.shawneepress.com

A NOTE FROM SHARON...

A few years ago, when Common Core was a new phrase in education circles, our school district was quick to study and adopt it. My administrator, a former all-state vocalist and music lover, would drop by my room and remark on how I was already incorporating Common Core into my music lessons, or how I could do so with an easy tweak to the existing lesson. My *Sticks!* book lessons are an example of what he observed, and eventually became a resource for others to use.

I spend my summers and several weekends presenting at workshops or facilitating professional development across the U.S. As I shared lessons from the *Sticks!* book and mentioned "Common Core," there was a recurring reaction of groans, head nods and looks of frustration. I met many music teachers whose administrators were requiring incorporation of the Common Core State Standards (CCSS) into their music curriculum without any explanation, training or instruction on the why, what or how to do so. Understandably, unless an administrator has a music education background, he or she is not sure how to guide a music teacher to meet the requirements.

Thus, this practical handbook is here to help, breaking the Common Core State Standards down into understandable bites, providing only the information a music teacher needs to successfully incorporate Common Core State Standards into existing music lesson plans—step-by-step. Like me, there is a good chance you are already including CCSS and just need to understand the code and how to articulate what you already do.

Teaching music first, incorporating the Common Core State Standards second, and when feasible.
--Sharon
www.CommonCoreinK5Music.com

DEDICATION

Dedicated to Scott Clark – an administrator who prioritized every decision with "what's best for kids," and led by example with a servant's heart.

ABOUT THE WRITER

Sharon Burch is a National Board Certified Teacher in Early and Middle Childhood Music, a certified teacher with the International Piano Teaching Foundation, and holds a master's degree as a Professional Educator. She authored the national best-selling interactive *Freddie the Frog Book series*, teaching resources, musicals, and jazz education teaching strategies for the classroom setting. Sharon serves on the international Jazz Education Network Education Committee, and serves as an elementary education consultant for Jazz At Lincoln Center.

www.SharonBurch.com
Kids: www.FreddieTheFrog.com
Music Teachers: www.TeachingWithFreddieTheFrog.com

TABLE OF CONTENTS

Your Common Core in Music implementation plan complete!

Help! I need to make sense of the Common Core and I have no time!

Music teachers are stretched to the limit in time and energy. On top of teaching music, the part that we love, we share the other responsibilities of our school districts. Recess duty, lunch duty, covering a class, requested performances, community events, and more, fill any extra down time. Then along comes the Common Core State Standards.

In many states, administrators are asking music teachers to understand and incorporate the Common Core State Standards (CCSS) into their music curriculum, or at least be aware of the CCSS and look for ways to do so. Yet, unless an administrator has a music education background, he or she is not sure how to advise or give guidance to the music teacher. Administrators are necessarily focusing on how to guide the classroom teachers due to his or her unique accountability to report to the district/state an effective implementation. Often times, the music teacher is asked to participate in Common Core State Standards Math or ELA professional development and adapt into the music classroom.

Sound familiar?

This practical handbook provides help when asked to incorporate the Common Core State Standards (CCSS) Math and/or ELA into your music classroom. The good news is that we are often already doing so, we just don't realize it or know how to articulate it effectively to our administrators. Chapters 1, 2 and 3 briefly explain what the Common Core State Standards are and how they function. Chapters 4 and 5 explain how you can incorporate and articulate to your administrator using the CCSS code. However, before we move forward, it helps to understand the "why" before addressing the "what" and "how."

The "Why"

A music teacher first; incorporating the Common Core second.

Why should you "have to" incorporate CCSS Math and/or ELA into your music classroom? Does this mean you need to put your music resources into the closet and begin teaching math and literacy? NO. No one is asking that. If they are, then it is even more important to take a proactive approach and understand the philosophy behind the Common Core, and demonstrate how incorporating it into music can work, without taking away from the learning of music. In fact, it often makes the learning richer. You are a music teacher first, incorporating the Common Core second.

If your administrator is requiring you to attend the professional development workshops, but not incorporate into your music classroom, I encourage you to do so anyway--when it makes sense. This will validate your music program in the eyes of non-music advocates. It will garner respect and your administrator will be grateful that you were able to develop a way to incorporate and articulate the Common Core in the music classroom, which he or she can report without additional headaches.

Chapter 1

Making Sense of the Common Core State Standards

You look at the time and scramble to check off two more things on your list before hurrying off to the teacher's meeting. You arrive to discover the focus of the gathering is how to implement Common Core State Standards for Math or English Language Arts. The speaker begins sharing strategies and sharing codes, and all of the general classroom teachers are scribbling notes and nodding their heads as though they all understand a secret language. You begin to zone out. Then you hear the speaker share that every teacher needs to incorporate the Common Core State Standards in their classroom—even the music teacher. What?! What about teaching music?

That could be the beginning of a philosophical debate. This book is not about the value of music education. That is a given. All children need and deserve a quality music education. Period. But if you are reading this book, I suspect your administrator has asked you to incorporate the Common Core State Standards (CCSS) in your music classroom. This book is a practical guide, sharing only what a music teacher needs to understand to incorporate the Common Core State Standards into K-5 Music.

How do we deal with continuing to teach music and meet the Common Core State Standards requirements that your administrator and district are asking of you? First, it helps to make sense of the Common Core State Standards and why they exist.

In years past, each state designed a set of standards for expected achievement. If children only lived in one location and worked in one region as an adult, the system worked. Times have changed.

Children move with their families from state to state on a regular basis. The expectations of student learning in one district/state varied from the other, positioning the re-locating child either ahead of the new class or behind, depending on which academic goals were emphasized in each location.

In addition, due to the Internet, ease of travel and other economic factors, we now compete globally in the workforce. In an effort to solve these problems, The Counsel of Chief State School Officers (CCSSO) and the National Governors Association (NGA) in 48 states came together to create a consistent set of standards that could be voluntarily adopted by each state—the Common Core State Standards.

Once you understand the system, then it becomes easy to find ways to incorporate the standards into what you already teach. Actually, most of us already include some of the standards; we just need to know how to document them in a way our administrator understands. This book will show you how.

◆ What are the Common Core State Standards?

The Common Core State Standards were written by answering the following questions.

"What do students need to understand and be able to do by the end of grade 12 to be college and career ready?"

"What do students need to understand and be able to do by the end of each grade level to achieve college and career readiness by high school graduation?"

The answers to those two questions are the Common Core State Standards. It shifts your planning from asking, "What do I need to teach to this year?" to "What do the students need to understand and be able to do by the end of this year?" The standards shift the instructional strategies from *teacher-driven to student-learner focused.* It's a simple, but important shift that impacts your teaching strategies, and more importantly, student learning in a positive way.

The Common Core State Standards consist of a combination of content and skills. Across the English language arts and mathematics standards, skills critical to each content area are emphasized. In particular, problem-solving, collaboration, communication and critical-thinking skills are interwoven into the standards.[1] *(Bold Emphasis added.)*

The Common Core State Standards for Mathematics include eight Mathematical Practice standards that apply to all grade levels in the instructional planning and learning of the grade-specific Mathematical Content.

The Common Core State Standards for English Language Arts/ Literacy include the College and Career Readiness Anchor Standards (CCRA or CCR), which serve as the broad standards guiding the grade-specific ELA-Literacy standards, encompassing knowledge in literature and other disciplines through the *four strands of reading, writing, speaking and listening, and language.*

---

1   http://www.corestandards.org/about-the-standards/frequently-asked-questions/#faq-2323

http://www.CoreStandards.org is the official website of the Common Core State Standards initiative, and serves as the resource and reference for the information throughout this book. The website hosts the official version of the standards, including a downloadable web version (XML format), a set of frequently asked questions, detailed information, writers' credentials, philosophy, and other related resources.

Common Core State Standards

Authors: National Governors Association (NGA) Center for Best Practices, Council of Chief State School Officers (CCSSO)

Publisher: National Governors Association Center for Best Practices, Council of Chief State School Officers, Washington, D.C.

The next chapter explains the structure and purpose of the Mathematical Practices and Mathematical Content.

WARNING: It is tempting to jump to the CCSS codes without looking at The Mathematical Practices (MP) and College and Career Ready Anchor Standards (CCRA). Don't do it! If you only focus on the CCSS content standards, then students only learn content with little or not skills for life application. The Mathematical Practices need to weave through the CCSS Mathematical Content, and the CCRA standards need to permeate the CCSS English Language Arts/Literacy for students to become academically independent and prepared. It will influence how you incorporate the CCSS into your music lesson plan. The combination actually makes the instruction better and the learning richer, including a richer music education.

◆ Additional Help

1. Watch the 3-minute animated video clip at: http://www.core-standards.org/ (Click on the video tab in the upper right.)

2. You can use this book and the charts independently. If you find you need additional assistance, the corresponding Common Core in K-5 Music Online Course walks you through the steps in this book in further detail. It is an independent 5-day course with instructional videos, making it easy to understand and swap lesson ideas with other teachers. http://www.CommonCoreinK5Music.com

CCSS Mathematics Standards

COMMON CORE STATE STANDARDS

Mathematics

Mathematical Practices
Apply K-12

MP1 Make sense of problems and persevere in solving them.
MP2 Reason abstractly and quantitatively.
MP3 Construct viable arguments and critique the reasoning of others.
MP4 Model with mathematics.
MP5 Use appropriate tools strategically.
MP6 Attend to precision.
MP7 Look for and make use of structure.
MP8 Look for and express regularity in repeated reasoning.

Mathematical Practices apply to all grade-specific Math Content Standards

Math Content Standards
Grade-Specific

- Counting and Cardinality (K)
- Operations & Algebraic Thinking (K-5)
- Number & Operations in Base Ten (K-5)
- Number & Operations – Fractions (3-5)
- Measurement & Data (K-5)
- Geometry (K-5)

Chapter 2

What are the CCSS for Mathematics?

◆ CCSS Mathematics Summary

CCSS Mathematics prepares students to think and reason mathematically, and to focus on developing a depth of understanding and ability to apply mathematics to novel situations, as college students and employees regularly do.[2]

Key shifts in Math:

- Greater **focus** on fewer topics, the major work, or critical areas per grade:

    K-5: whole numbers, addition, subtraction, multiplication, division, fractions, and decimals.

- **Coherence**: Linking topics and thinking across grades.
- **Rigor**: Pursue conceptual understanding, procedural skills and fluency, and application with equal intensity.

List and detailed explanation of Key Shifts located at: http://www.corestandards.org/other-resources/key-shifts-in-mathematics/

---

2   P. 5, *K-8 Publishers criteria for the Common Core State Standards for Mathematics*
http://achievethecore.org/page/266/k-8-publishers-criteria-for-the-common-core-state-standards-for-mathematics

◆ Apply Mathematical Practices at every grade level.

MP1 Make sense of problems and persevere in solving them.
MP2 Reason abstractly and quantitatively.
MP3 Construct viable arguments and critique the reasoning of others.
MP4 Model with mathematics.
MP5 Use appropriate tools strategically.
MP6 Attend to precision.
MP7 Look for and make use of structure.
MP8 Look for and express regularity in repeated reasoning.

Detailed additional information located at:
http://www.corestandards.org/Math/Practice/

◆ Grade-Specific Mathematical Content

Incorporate grade-specific Mathematical Content combined with Mathematical Practices standards into music lessons when applicable.
- Understand the grade-specific critical areas (See grade level Introduction pages).
- Understand the grade-specific Math Standards.
  - CCSS Math organized by domain, then clusters.

Read through the specific CCSS Math standards per grade level at:
http://www.corestandards.org/Math/

Is your head spinning?

If the Mathematics Summary left your head spinning, below is additional information to help break it down. Remember, complete detailed explanations and information located at www. CoreStandards.com.

◆ What are Focus, Coherence and Rigor?

Include focus, coherence and rigor in instructional strategies. For the purpose of understanding the idea behind these three words, here's a simplified example to illustrate Mathematical Content without focus, coherence and rigor.

Pretend a student learns how to add and subtract, and practices ninety-nine addition and subtraction computations with great success (Mathematical Content), earning the highest score at the end of the year. That summer, the same student walks to the local store with a dollar bill to purchase a candy bar that costs $.75. The student discovers that a piece of gum costs $.30 and wonders if he or she has enough money to buy both. Even though the student can add and subtract very well, the student did not have any coherence, rigor or relevance when learning to add and subtract. He or she had no idea how to solve the relevant, real-world problem.

The example illustrates the reason for instructional planning to begin with the question, ***"What do the students need to understand and be able to do by the end of the year?"*** Begin with a relevant story problem that causes the student to think through how he or she would need to solve the problem. This creates relevance, or a reason, to learn how to add and subtract, or another content skill, in order to solve the problem.

FOCUS on the critical areas of each grade level. Refer to the grade level critical areas first and look for ways to incorporate it in your lesson, applying the mathematical practices when appropriate. Each grade level lists critical areas in the introduction.

COHERANCE is about making math make sense. Mathematics is not a list of disconnected tricks or mnemonics. The Standards define progressions of learning as they build knowledge in content and mathematical practices over the grades.

RIGOR is about pursuing with equal intensity in the major work of each grade, or critical area.
- Conceptual understanding
- Procedural skill and fluency, and
- Applications[3]

The phrase "rigor and relevance," often heard in general classroom education sessions, correlates to the above.

---

3   P. 3 *K-8 Publishers criteria for the Common Core State Standards for Mathematics*
     http://achievethecore.org/page/266/k-8-publishers-criteria-for-the-common-core-state-standards-for-mathematics

Read through this section again, but with music content in mind. We already apply all of these things! They are inherent to music instruction. This book will give you the Common Core State Standard codes to articulate and report what we already do in the music classroom, and look for ways to incorporate math when appropriate.

◆ Mathematical Practices Standards

Apply to all grade levels, K-12

The CCSS Math standards are a combination of Math Practice and Content Standards to develop mathematical thinking. The Mathematical Practices standards guide the implementation of focus, coherence and rigor in the CCSS for Mathematics.

The 8 Mathematical Practices Standards

> MP1 Make sense of problems and persevere in solving them.
>
> MP2 Reason abstractly and quantitatively.
>
> MP3 Construct viable arguments and critique the reasoning of others.
>
> MP4 Model with mathematics.
>
> MP5 Use appropriate tools strategically.
>
> MP6 Attend to precision.
>
> MP7 Look for and make use of structure.
>
> MP8 Look for and express regularity in repeated reasoning.

- Read through the Mathematical Practices Standards in detail at: http://www.corestandards.org/Math/Practice/
- Read through the standards a second time, with music content in mind. It is easy to find an instructional correlation. Again, we already use adaptations of many of these practices in our music instruction.

Guiding questions and problem solving become the heart of instructional strategies. This creates rigor, relevance, coherence and enduring understanding for the student. Questions and problem solving develop students' conceptual understanding of key concepts. The student leaves the classroom empowered thinking, "I can solve that problem." Thus, creating "I can" statements for lesson plan objectives aligns well with the Common Core.

Guiding questions and facilitation of procedural learning include:

1. Conceptual questions

2. Classroom discussion to engage in mathematical practices such as constructing and critiquing arguments (MP.3)

3. Solving equations as a process of answering questions

4. Computation, including knowing single-digit products and sums from memory (see, e.g., 2.OA.2 and 3.OA.7)[4]

This summary from the *K-8 Publishers Criteria for the Common Core State Standards for Mathematics* easily adapts to music as well as math. The lessons that I structure with these thoughts in mind, end up being the best lessons in which you can almost hear the wheels turning in students' minds. The understanding is deep and enduring beyond the allotted class time.

> Lessons are thoughtfully structured and support the teacher in leading the class through the learning paths at hand, with active participation by all students in their own learning and in the learning of their classmates. Teachers are supported in extending student explanations and modeling explanations of new methods. Lesson structure frequently calls for students to find solutions to explain their reasoning, and ask and answer question about their reasoning as it concerns problems, diagrams, mathematical models, etc. Over time there is a rhythm back and

---

4   *K-8 Publishers criteria for the Common Core State Standards for Mathematics*
     http://achievethecore.org/page/266/k-8-publishers-criteria-for-the-common-core-state-standards-for-mathematics

forth between making sense of concepts and exercising for proficiency.[5]

Students are asked to produce answers and solutions, but also, in a grade-appropriate way, arguments, explanations, diagrams, mathematical models, etc. In a way appropriate to the grade level, students are asked to answer questions or develop explanations about why a solution makes sense, how quantities are represented in expressions, and how elements of symbolic, diagrammatic, tabular, graphical and /or verbal representations correspond.[6]

Manipulatives and concrete representations are recommended, such as diagrams and physical objects that connect to written and symbolic notation. A similar application can be adapted to music analysis, composition, notation, etc. Like learning any language, we learn by using it. We already understand this in the music classroom.

Often times, you can incorporate a math concept by how you phrase a question while teaching music. The lessons in the book, *Sticks!* (Hal Leonard Corporation), are created on this premise. The craft sticks double as a manipulative for music and math, but more on that later!

◆ Additional Tips to Keep in Mind

- Use correct mathematical vocabulary for consistency and understanding.
- "Problems" refer to something that a student is learning how to solve, not a calculation. Problems progressively build understanding through the process of solving them.
- "Exercises" refer to a practice exercise to build fluency, such as multiplication facts.

---

5   P. 19, *K-8 Publishers criteria for the Common Core State Standards for Mathematics*
http://achievethecore.org/page/266/k-8-publishers-criteria-for-the-common-core-state-standards-for-mathematics
6   P. 16, *K-8 Publishers criteria for the Common Core State Standards for Mathematics*
http://achievethecore.org/page/266/k-8-publishers-criteria-for-the-common-core-state-standards-for-mathematics

The 8 Mathematical Practices apply to all grade levels in the instructional planning and learning of the grade-specific **Mathematical Content.**

◆ Mathematical Content Standards

Grade-Level Specific

The Mathematical Content Standards are the grade-specific Common Core State Standards for Math, in which you apply the Mathematical Practices grade-level appropriately, as briefly described above, and in detail at the website, http://www.corestandards.org/Math/Practice/.

The K-5 Mathematics Content standards lay a solid foundation in:

- Whole numbers
- Addition
- Subtraction
- Multiplication
- Division
- Fractions
- Decimals

The Mathematical Content Standards are organized in the following domains:

- Counting and Cardinality (K)
- Operations & Algebraic Thinking (K-5)
- Number & Operations in Base Ten (K-5)
- Number & Operations – Fractions (3-5)
- Measurement & Data (K-5)
- Geometry (K-5)

Locate and read through the specific CCSS Math standards per grade level in the appendix or at: http://www.corestandards.org/Math/

How to Read the Grade-Specific Math Content Standards

1. **Read the grade-specific Critical Areas first.** Critical areas are located at the top of the "Grade K Math Standards" in the appendix of this book, and on each grade level's introduction page at the website. For example, the Kindergarten critical areas are located in the first paragraph at: http://www.core-standards.org/Math/Content/K/introduction/ When you read through the content standards of each grade level, it is easy to feel overwhelmed. **Remember, you are a music teacher first.** Look for ways to incorporate the critical areas. If you happen to incorporate other content standards, that is fine, but the critical areas are priority.

2. **Read the grade-specific Content Standards in each domain.** "Grade K Math Standards" are located in the appendix of this book, on the digital download charts, and on the website. For example, if planning a Kindergarten lesson, click on "Kindergarten" in the gold column on the right at the website, or read the Kindergarten Math Chart in the appendix.

   - Domains: Click on each domain underneath a grade level to see the grade-specific standards for each domain.
   - Clusters: Groups of standards are organized in clusters underneath each domain.

🛑 STOP

   - Read through the Mathematical Content Standards Introduction in detail at: http://www.corestandards.org/Math/
     1. Click on "Read the Standards" at the website.
     2. Click on "Mathematics Standards."
     3. Click on the "Introduction" located on the right in the gold column.

4. Click on the "Introduction" located underneath each grade level to locate and read the critical areas.

5. Read through the Mathematics Content standards of the youngest grade level you teach. For example, if kindergarten is the youngest grade level you teach, do the following:

   - Click on http://www.corestandards.org/Math/.

   - In the gold column on the right side of the website page, click on "Kindergarten."

   - Click on the each of the domains in the drop-down list below kindergarten and read the text on the left in the white area for each of the domains.

   - As you read through the standards for the youngest grade level you teach, think about music lessons that could incorporate the standards.

   - Write/record ideas and the corresponding codes that come to mind.

Is it beginning to make sense?

This book serves as a shortcut, or practical guide. Detailed explanations and information are located at www.CoreStandards.com.

◆ Additional Help

The corresponding Common Core in K-5 Music Online Course includes videos with screenshots of the website and step-by-step instructions on how to navigate the www.CoreStandards.org website, and make sense of the Mathematical Practice Standards, and Grade-Level Critical Areas and Content Standards. http://www.CommonCoreinK5Music.com

CCSS ELA/Literacy Standards

COMMON CORE STATE STANDARDS

English Language Arts/Literacy

College and Career Readiness Anchor Standards K-12

- Reading
- Writing
- Speaking & Listening
- Language

CCR Anchor Standards apply to all grade-specific ELA/Literacy

ELA Standards
Grade-Specific

- Reading
  - Literature
  - Informational Text
  - Foundational Skills
- Writing
- Speaking & Listening
- Language

Chapter 3

What Are the ELA/Literacy Standards?

◆ College and Career Readiness Anchor Standards

Apply to all grade levels, K-12

The College and Career Readiness Anchor Standards (CCRA or CCR) for English Language Arts/Literacy provide the broad understanding and purpose for the grade-specific standards. Although you will most likely document the grade-specific Common Core State Standard ELA/Literacy incorporated into your music lesson plan, reading through the Anchor Standards will bring understanding of why the grade-specific standard exists and the end goal for its existence. They provide context for the specific standards, making it easier to create strategies to incorporate specific standards. Read the CCR in the appendix or at www.CoreStandards.org.

Four Strands

Reading: Text complexity and the growth of comprehension

- Key Ideas and Details
- Craft and Structure
- Integration of Knowledge and Ideas
- Range of Reading and Level of Text Complexity

Writing: Text types, responding to reading, and research

- Text Types and Purposes
- Production and Distribution of Writing
- Research to Build and Present Knowledge
- Range of Writing

Speaking and Listening: Flexible communication and collaboration

- Comprehension and Collaboration
- Presentation of Knowledge and Ideas

Language: Conventions, effective use and vocabulary

- Conventions of Standard English
- Knowledge of Language
- Vocabulary Acquisition and Use

(STOP)

Read through the College and Career Readiness Anchor Standards in detail at: http://www.corestandards.org/ELA-Literacy/

1. Click on the "Introduction" in the gold column on the right and read the information in the white area on the left side in detail.

2. Click on "Anchor Standards" in the gold column on the right and read each strand in detail.

3. Read through the standards a second time, with music content in mind. It is easy to find an instructional correlation. Again, we already use adaptations of many of these standards in our music instruction.
   - Vocal music includes text, making it easy to incorporate many ELA/Literacy standards.
   - When treating music notation as text, applying the standards allows for a richer learning experience, although not directly applicable for reporting CCSS purposes.

◆ Additional Help

The corresponding Common Core in K-5 Music Online Course includes videos with screenshots of the website, step-by-step instructions on how to navigate the www.CoreStandards.org website, and make sense of the College and Career Readiness Standards. http://www.CommonCoreinK5Music.com

◆ ELA/Literacy Standards

Grade-Level Specific

Each of the four strands further break down, grouping each standard together, to detail grade-level specific ELA/Literacy standards.

Reading: Grade-specific text complexity and the growth of comprehension organized in three subgroups:

> Reading: Literature
> Reading: Informational Text
> Reading: Foundational Skills

Writing: Grade-specific text types, responding to reading and research

Speaking and Listening: Grade-specific flexible communication and collaboration

Language: Grade-specific conventions, effective use and vocabulary

- Read the ELA/Literacy Standards of the **youngest grade level you teach** on the digital download charts, or at the official website. As you read through the ELA/Literacy standards for the youngest grade level you teach, think about music lessons that could incorporate the standards.
- Write/record ideas and the corresponding codes that come to mind. For example, if kindergarten is the youngest grade level you teach, read: http://www.corestandards.org/ELA-Literacy/RL/K/

1. Click on "Reading: Literature" in the gold column on the right.

2. Click on "Kindergarten" below "Reading: Literature" in the gold column on the right and read in detail.

3. Click on "Reading: Informational Text" in the gold column on the right.

4. Click on "Kindergarten" below "Reading: Informational Text" in the gold column on the right and read in detail.

5. Click on "Reading: Foundational Skills" in the gold column on the right.

6. Click on "Kindergarten" below "Reading: Foundational Skills" in the gold column on the right and read in detail.

7. Click on "Writing" in the gold column on the right.

8. Click on "Kindergarten" below "Writing" in the gold column on the right and read in detail.

9. Click on "Speaking & Listening" in the gold column on the right.

10. Click on "Kindergarten" below "Speaking & Listening" in the gold column on the right and read in detail.

11. Click on "Language" in the gold column on the right.

12. Click on "Kindergarten" below "Language" in the gold column on the right and read in detail.

Is it beginning to make sense?

◆ **Additional Help**

The corresponding Common Core in K-5 Music Online Course includes videos with screenshots of the website and step-by-step instructions on how to navigate the www.CoreStandards.org website, and commentary on how to make sense of the English Language Arts/Literacy Standards. http://www.CommonCoreinK-5Music.com

Your district requirements will determine the extent you include all of the strands in your music classroom.

- **The Reading, and Speaking and Listening strands are easiest to incorporate** in the purist CCSS ELA/Literacy sense, especially when focusing on the text in vocal music.
- The processes of the writing and language strands can easily be adapted and applied to music notation and composition, although not directly related to the CCSS ELA/Literacy skills and content standards.

Regardless, combining instructional strategies for English and Music as languages meets the requirements of the district while making the learning of music richer, reinforcing the processes developed in students.

The following points from The James B Hunt, Jr. Institute for Educational Leadership and Policy "CCSS Briefing Packet" 21-page PDF document are helpful to read as you seek ways to incorporate the ELA/Literacy standards:

> ELA critical content for all students, including, but not limited to:
> - Classic myths and stories from around the world
> - America's founding documents
> - Foundational American literature
> - Shakespeare[7]

Folk songs and stories from around the globe, along with patriotic music and songs, already exist in K-5 general music classrooms. Incorporating ELA/Literacy into your lesson plans is easy once you are familiar with the standards for each grade level.

Here are some additional notes from The James B Hunt, Jr. Institute for Educational Leadership and Policy "CCSS Briefing Packet" 21-page PDF document.

---

7   P. 10, http://www.hunt-institute.org/elements/media/files/CCSS_Briefing_Packet.pdf

The remaining crucial decisions about what content should be taught are made at the state and local levels.

- Recognition that both content and skills are important.
- Balance between fiction/literature and non-fiction/ biography/informational texts.[8]
- Students are expected to research and utilize media in all content areas.[9]

The authors of the Common Core State Standards recognized the need for an increased emphasis on informational text in grades K-12. Look for opportunities in music to incorporate information- al text when appropriate, such as biographical text about compos- ers and artists, or instruments, culture, etc. Also notice the third bullet point of student expectations to research and utilize media in all content areas, music included. Again, this is fairly easy to do in the subject of music.

The official CCSS website explains the purpose and design of the English Language Arst(ELA)/Literacy Standards in detail. http:// www.corestandards.org/ELA-Literacy/

---

8   P. 10, http://www.hunt-institute.org/elements/media/files/CCSS_Briefing_Packet.pdf
9   P. 9, http://www.hunt-institute.org/elements/media/files/CCSS_Briefing_Packet.pdf

◆ Frequently Asked Questions and Answers from www.CoreStandards.org

Will CCSSO and the NGA Center be creating common instructional materials and curricula?

> No. The standards are not curricula and do not mandate the use of any particular curriculum. **Teachers are able to develop their own lesson plans and choose materials, as they have always done. States that have adopted the standards may choose to work together to develop instructional materials and curricula.** As states work individually to implement their new standards, publishers of instructional materials and experienced educators will develop new resources around these shared standards.

Are there data collection requirements associated with the Common Core State Standards?

> No. Implementing the Common Core State Standards does not require data collection. **Standards define expectations for what students should know and be able to do by the end of each grade. The means of assessing students and the data that result from those assessments are up to the discretion of each state and are separate and unique from the Common Core.**[10] *(Bold Emphasis added.)*

Both of these points are good news for music educators, allowing flexibility and creativity in *how* we incorporate the CCSS standards into our music classroom.

---

10   http://www.corestandards.org/about-the-standards/frequently-asked-questions/

Understanding the CCSS Code

Now that you understand the overall picture, it makes understanding the codes easy. If you have followed the instructions in the previous chapters to stop and read through standards, you probably understand the structure of the Common Core State Standards coding system. Using the CCSS codes serve as a communication tool for tracking, reporting and communicating with your administrator and colleagues in the general classroom. A majority of the time, you will use the grade-specific codes, but it is important to understand the broad standard codes. The Mathematical Practices Standards and the College and Career Readiness Anchor Standards for ELA/Literacy serve as the broader goals in which the content standards align.

CCSS Mathematics Codes

COMMON CORE STATE STANDARDS

Mathematics

CCSS Codes

CCSS.MATH.PRACTICE.MP1 Make sense of problems and persevere in solving them.
CCSS.MATH.PRACTICE.MP2 Reason abstractly and quantitatively.
CCSS.MATH.PRACTICE.MP3 Construct viable arguments and critique the reasoning of others.
CCSS.MATH.PRACTICE.MP4 Model with mathematics.
CCSS.MATH.PRACTICE.MP5 Use appropriate tools strategically.
CCSS.MATH.PRACTICE.MP6 Attend to precision.
CCSS.MATH.PRACTICE.MP7 Look for and make use of structure.
CCSS.MATH.PRACTICE.MP8 Look for and express regularity in repeated reasoning.

↓ *Mathematical Practices apply to all grade-specific Math Content Standards* ↓

Math Content Standards Domains

Domains per grade level: *indicates grade level*

CCSS.MATH.CONTENT.K.CC Counting and Cardinality
CCSS.MATH.CONTENT.K.OA Operations & Algebraic Thinking
CCSS.MATH.CONTENT.K.NBT Number & Operations in Base Ten
CCSS.MATH.CONTENT.K.NF   Number & Operations - Fractions
CCSS.MATH.CONTENT.K.MD Measurement & Data
CCSS.MATH.CONTENT.K.G   Geometry

Example of a grade-specific CCSS Math Standard:
CCSS.MATH.CONTENT.K.CC.A.1

◆ Understanding the CCSS Mathematical Practice Code

Example code: **CCSS.MATH.PRACTICE.MP1**

Code represents: **C**ommon **C**ore **S**tate **S**tandards.**Math**ematics.
Practice standards.**M**athematical **P**ractice standard **#1**

Example abbreviation of the same code: **MP1**

Apply the CCSS for Mathematical Practice at every grade level.
Details and explanations located at: http://www.corestandards.
org/Math/Practice/

CCSS.MATH.PRACTICE.MP1
Make sense of problems and persevere in solving them.

CCSS.MATH.PRACTICE.MP2
Reason abstractly and quantitatively.

CCSS.MATH.PRACTICE.MP3
Construct viable arguments and critique the reasoning of others.

CCSS.MATH.PRACTICE.MP4
Model with mathematics.

CCSS.MATH.PRACTICE.MP5
Use appropriate tools strategically.

CCSS.MATH.PRACTICE.MP6
Attend to precision.

CCSS.MATH.PRACTICE.MP7
Look for and make use of structure.

CCSS.MATH.PRACTICE.MP8
Look for and express regularity in repeated reasoning.

◆ Understanding the CCSS Mathematical Content Code

Example code: **CCSS.MATH.CONTENT.K.CC.A.1**

Code represents: **C**ommon **C**ore **S**tate **S**tandard.**Math**ematics.
Content (not Practice).**K**indergarten.**C**ounting and **C**ardinality
(domain).**A** (cluster).**1** (specific standard)

CCSS	=	Common Core State Standard
MATH	=	Mathematics
CONTENT	=	Content standard (not Practice standard)
K	=	Kindergarten grade-specific standard
CC	=	Counting and Cardinality domain group
A	=	Specified Cluster underneath a specific domain.
1	=	Specific standard number in domain (Note: Standard numbers remain in sequence throughout the domain.)

A diagram of how to read the CCSS Math Standards located at:
http://www.corestandards.org/Math/Content/introduction/how-to-read-the-grade-level-standards/

Standards Abbreviations

Your school district may use an abbreviation of this system for
recording/reporting.

For example, some districts would report the above math standard only using the following to reference the same standard:
MATH.K.CC.1

Other common Standards abbreviations:

3.MD.7 = an individual content standard *(Grade 3.MD=Measurement & Data.number 7)*

MP.8 = a practice standard *(MP=Mathematical Practice standard 8)*

4.NBT = a domain heading *(Grade 4.NBT=Number & Operations in Base 10)*

Check with your administrator for his or her preference.

◆ Common Core State Standard Resources

The official website is the best and most complete resource for codes and definitions. Once you understand the structure of the CCSS, the mobile device App is handy to have at your fingertips.

Official website: www.CoreStandards.org

App: CommonCore (Powered by MasteryConnect. www.MasteryConnect.com)

Digital download includes Common Core State Standards charts and lesson planning templates. A reduced image of the charts and templates located in Appendix A.

CCSS Language Arts/Literacy Codes

COMMON CORE STATE STANDARDS

ELA/Literacy CCSS Codes

College and Career Readiness Anchor Standards K-12

CCSS.ELA-LITERACY.CCRA.R.	Reading
CCSS.ELA-LITERACY.CCRA.W.	Writing
CCSS.ELA-LITERACY.CCRA.SL.	Speaking & Listening
CCSS.ELA-LITERACY.CCRA.L.	Language

CCR Anchor Standards apply to all grade-specific ELA/Literacy

ELA Standards Grade-Specific

Domains per grade level:
Reading:

Reading: Literature	CCSS.ELA-LITERACY.RL.
Reading: Informational Text	CCSS.ELA-LITERACY.RI.
Reading: Foundational Skills	CCSS.ELA-LITERACY.RF.
Writing	CCSS.ELA-LITERACY.W.
Speaking & Listening	CCSS.ELA-LITERACY.SL.
Language	CCSS.ELA-LITERACY.L.

Example of a CCSS ELA/Literacy grade-specific Code:
CCSS.ELA-LITERACY.RL.K.1
— *indicates grade level*

◆ Understanding the CCSS ELA/Literacy Codes

College and Career Readiness Anchor Standards

There are four strands of College and Career Readiness Anchor Standards for English Language Arts/Literacy:

- CCSS.ELA-LITERACY.CCRA.R = **Reading**
- CCSS.ELA-LITERACY.CCRA.W = **Writing**
- CCSS.ELA-LITERACY.CCRA.SL = **Speaking & Listening**
- CCSS.ELA-LITERACY.CCRA.L = **Language**

Example: **CCSS.ELA-LITERACY.CCRA.R.1**

Code represents: **C**ommon **C**ore **S**tate **S**tandards.**E**nglish Language **A**rts-**Literacy**.**C**ollege and **C**areer **R**eady **A**nchor.**R**eading.**1**

$$
\begin{aligned}
\text{CCSS} &= \text{Common Core State Standards} \\
\text{ELA} &= \text{English Language Arts} \\
\text{CCRA} &= \text{College and Career Ready Anchor (Standards)} \\
\text{R} &= \text{Reading Strand} \\
1 &= \text{Specific standard \#1}
\end{aligned}
$$

◆ Understanding the Grade-Specific CCSS ELA/Literacy Codes

These are the codes you will most likely record and report.

> **The same strands break down in further detail for the grade-specific ELA/Literacy standards.**

Notice that the CCRA portion of the code is no longer included. Instead, the specific strand, followed by grade level and specific standard number, replaces it. Grade level Kindergarten and standard 1 are used in the following examples.

- CCSS.ELA-LITERACY.**RL**.K.1 = Reading: Literature
- CCSS.ELA-LITERACY.**RI**.K.1 = Reading: Informational Text
- CCSS.ELA-LITERACY.**RF**.K.1 = Reading: Foundational Skills
- CCSS.ELA-LITERACY.**W**.K.1 = Writing
- CCSS.ELA-LITERACY.**SL**.K.1 = Speaking & Listening
- CCSS.ELA-LITERACY.**L** .K.1 = Language

Example: **CCSS.ELA-LITERACY.RL.K.1**

Code represents: **C**ommon **C**ore **S**tate **S**tandard.**E**nglish **L**anguage **A**rts-**Literacy**.**R**eading:Literature (domain).**K**indergarten.**1** (standard #1 in the domain)

CCSS = Common Core State Standards
ELA/Literacy = English Language Arts/Literacy
RL = Reading: Literature strand
K = Kindergarten grade-specific standard
1 = Standard #1

Possible abbreviated code example: **ELA.RL.K.1**

Check with your administrator for his or her preference.

◆ Common Core State Standard Resources

The official website is the best and most complete resource for codes and definitions. Once you understand the structure of the CCSS, the mobile device App is handy to have at your fingertips.

Official website: www.CoreStandards.org

App: CommonCore (Powered by MasteryConnect. www.MasteryConnect.com)

Digital download includes Common Core State Standards charts and lesson planning templates. A reduced image of the charts and templates located in Appendix B.

You made it!

Explore the www.CoreStandards.org and apply to your music lessons. The following pages are example lessons with the CCSS standards incorporated and documented in a chart.

How to Incorporate CCSS into the Music Classroom

You are a music teacher first, incorporating Common Core State Standards second. As you explore ways to incorporate CCSS into music, it is easy to become overwhelmed with the amount of standards listed per grade level. Don't worry. It is not your job to include every standard listed. **It is your job (and passion) to teach music first and look for ways to incorporate CCSS when appropriate.**

There is no avoiding reading the Mathematical Practice Standards, College and Career Anchor Standards for ELA/Literacy, and the Common Core State Standards for the grade levels you teach. In order to know when it is appropriate to incorporate CCSS, you need a general understanding and awareness of the standards. **If you skipped to chapter 5, go back.** The previous chapters serve as a shortcut in understanding their purpose and structure. The www.CoreStandards.org website and CommonCore app are easy to navigate if you understand the structure explained in the previous chapters.

Remember, the standards state *what* students need to learn, not *how* to teach.

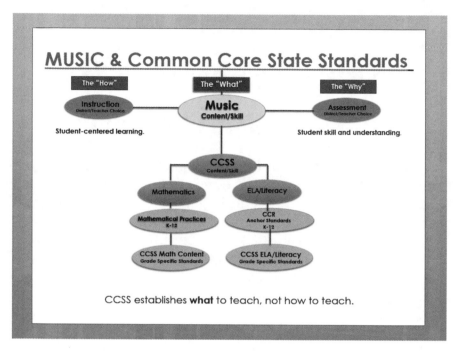

MUSIC & Common Core State Standards

The "How" — Instruction (District/Teacher Choice) — Student-centered learning.

The "What" — Music Content/Skill

The "Why" — Assessment (District/Teacher Choice) — Student skill and understanding.

CCSS Content/Skill
- Mathematics
  - Mathematical Practices K-12
  - CCSS Math Content Grade Specific Standards
- ELA/Literacy
  - CCR Anchor Standards K-12
  - CCSS ELA/Literacy Grade Specific Standards

CCSS establishes **what** to teach, not how to teach.

◆ How to Use Your Existing Music Lesson Plans to Incorporate CCSS

Do not throw out your existing lesson plans to incorporate CCSS. Once you have read through the CCSS grade level standards, read through your existing lesson plans looking for opportunities to include a standard or two by asking an additional question, or adding one or two steps to the lesson. (Examples of this are located at www.TeachingwithFreddieTheFrog.com lesson plans.) Before you begin the process, visit with your administrator and classroom teachers to gather additional information to make your job easier, and the learning connections easier for your students.

◆ What to Look for in Your School District's Curriculum and Resources

Each grade level general classroom will include specific literature, non-fiction books, and topics every year. They may already be listed in a curriculum guide or in the teacher notes. Being aware of that list makes it easy for you to plan when to incorporate a few titles into your music classroom.

Schedule time to ask your administrator or the classroom teachers the following questions regarding the grade levels you teach:

1. Kindergarten teacher specific: Do you have an outline of which colors, sounds, numbers, etc. are introduced when? May I have a copy?

2. What storybooks do you use in the classroom every year?

3. What nonfiction books do you use in the classroom every year?

4. What literature and chapter books do you use in the classroom every year?

5. What science and social studies topics or units do you cover each year?

6. What math manipulatives do you use in the classroom? (colored cubes, other?) Ask to borrow a few to make the connections in music.

7. What concepts of money, measurement, graphing, etc. do you cover? Ask to see samples of graphing familiar to students. Use something similar when appropriate in music or teach the correlation.

8. What American literature, poems, songs, etc., do you include?

For example, I love using the storybook, *Brown Bear, Brown Bear.* The students light up when they see a familiar story from their classroom. It is an easy story to add musical elements and review/extend Common Core standards. (Lesson details shared later in the chapter.)

American poems and literature are a natural correlation to patriotic songs, music and American folksongs. Learning these songs will be richer when incorporating English language standards that focus on the content, context, rhyming words, culture, etc.

◆ K-5 Common Core Charts to Use With Your Existing Lesson Plans

The digital download code, located on the first page, gives you access to these charts for your convenience. (See Appendixes A & B.) You can see standards at a glance while you create lesson plans. Download the digital CCSS charts as a printed or digital reference when planning lessons. Refer to www.CoreStandards.org for details.

- K-5 overview charts show the coherence and continuity at a glance.
- K-5 Grade Level charts include the specific codes in Math and ELA.

Create a Common Core State Standards reference notebook.

Use a ½" three-ring binder. Download and print the CCSS charts. Place charts in page protectors for convenient reference when planning lessons.

Scan the CCSS Math and ELA grade-specific charts to align with appropriate grade level focus. Record the CCSS codes you choose to develop in your instructional strategies.

◆ How to Create a Music Lesson Plan With Math Standards

1. **Read the Mathematical Practices**, which apply to every grade level, then read the following before creating a lesson plan.

2. **Read the critical areas of each grade level first** to understand the major work of each specific grade. These are listed in the first paragraph of each grade level's introduction page. *For example, the Kindergarten critical areas are located in the first paragraph at:* http://www.corestandards.org/Math/Content/K/introduction/

3. **Read the grade level Content Standards in each domain.** For example, if planning a Kindergarten lesson, click on "Kindergarten" in the gold column on the right. All of the Kindergarten CCSS Math Standards will appear on the left.
   - **Domains:** Click on each domain underneath a grade level to see the grade-specific standards for each domain.
   - **Clusters:** They are organized in clusters. Each cluster is represented by a letter.

4. **Review the Mathematical Practices to create the instructional strategies** that will include focus, coherence, and rigor in student learning in the lesson.

5. **Write down the Content Standard codes that you plan to use** in your music lesson.

6. **Look for teaching strategy ideas and lesson examples** in published books and on the Internet. Common Core State Standard resources are available on several websites.
   One of my favorite resources for getting ideas is located at: http://www.ixl.com/. It is organized well and the examples are easy to understand.

7. **Look for Music Lesson Plans with Common Core incorporated.** Beginning with my *Sticks!* book, each teacher's book and lesson plan that I create will include the CCSS codes listed at the end. *Math Rocks* (Hal Leonard Corporation) incorpo-

rates Common Core Math Standards. www.TeachingWith-FreddieTheFrog.com incorporates the standards in lessons that I love.

"I Can" Statements and Common Core State Standards

"I Can" statements work seamlessly with the Common Core State Standards. Student learning outcomes and expectations written as "I can" statements shift the paradigm from "teacher-driven" learning to "student-centered" learning. Each of the Common Core State Standards can easily be adapted to "I can" statements, as shown in the following 5th grade example.

Common Core State Standard
CCSS.MATH.CONTENT.5.OA.A.1
Use parentheses, brackets, or braces in numerical expressions, and evaluate expressions with these symbols.

"I Can" statement formulated using the same standard:
I can use parentheses, brackets, or braces in numerical expressions and evaluate expressions with these symbols.

Each standard can be converted into an "I can" statement by changing the first letter to lower case, and adding "I can" at the beginning of the standard.

Recording/Reporting Your
Common Core Implementation in Music
The digital download code, located on the first page, includes lesson plan templates with Common Core State Standard charts at the end for recording and reporting your CCSS implementation. In addition, a spreadsheet for documenting standards implemented per lesson is included.

◆ How to Create a Music Lesson Plan With ELA/Literacy Standards

The Common Core State Standards for English Language Arts are the grade-specific standards that lead to the College and Career Readiness Anchor Standards. Together, they form the CCSS.

1. **Read the College and Career Readiness Anchor Standards,** which apply to every grade level.
   - College and Career Readiness Anchor Standard for **Reading**
   - College and Career Readiness Anchor Standard for **Writing**
   - College and Career Readiness Anchor Standard for **Speaking & Listening**
   - College and Career Readiness Anchor Standard for **Language**
2. **Read each of the strands of the specific grade level.**
   - **Click on the strand** in the gold column on the right.
   - A drop down list of each grade level appears underneath each of the strands.
     - Reading: Literature
     - Reading: Informational Text
     - Reading: Foundational Skills
     - Writing
     - Speaking & Listening
     - Language
   - **Click on the specific grade level.**
3. **Read the grade level standards in each strand.** For example, if planning a Kindergarten lesson, click on "Kindergarten" in the gold column on the right. All of the Kindergarten Standards of the chosen strand will appear on the left.

4. **Write down the Standard codes you plan to use in your music lesson.**

5. **Look for teaching strategy ideas and lesson examples** in published books and on the Internet. Common Core State Standard resources are available on several websites.

> One of my favorite resources for getting ideas is located at: http://www.ixl.com/
>
> It is organized well and the examples are easy to understand.

6. **Look for Music Lesson Plans with Common Core incorporated**. Beginning with my *Sticks!* book, each teacher's book and lesson plan that I create will include the CCSS codes listed at the end. *Grammar Rocks* (Hal Leonard Corporation) includes Common Core ELA Standards. www.TeachingWithFreddieTheFrog.com incorporates the standards in lessons that I love.

"I Can" Statements and Common Core State Standards

"I Can" statements work seamlessly with the Common Core State Standards. Student learning outcomes and expectations written as "I can" statements shift the paradigm from "teacher-driven" learning to "student-centered" learning. Each of the Common Core State Standards can easily be adapted to "I can" statements, as shown in the following 5th grade example.

Common Core State Standard
CCSS.MATH.CONTENT.5.OA.A.1
Use parentheses, brackets, or braces in numerical expressions, and evaluate expressions with these symbols.

"I Can" statement formulated using the same standard:
I can use parentheses, brackets, or braces in numerical expressions and evaluate expressions with these symbols.

Each standard can be converted into an "I can" statement by changing the first letter to lower case, and adding "I can" at the beginning of the standard.

Recording/Reporting Your Common Core Implementation in Music

The digital download code, located on the first page, gives you access to lesson plan templates with Common Core State Standard charts at the end for recording and reporting your CCSS implementation. In addition, a spreadsheet for documenting standards implemented per lesson is included. (See Appendix C.)

Look for opportunities to incorporate CCSS Math and ELA/ Literacy Standards in the same music lesson.

◆ Example: K-2 Music Lesson with CCSS That Incorporates Math Standards

The following lesson is a detailed, step-by-step excerpt from the *Sticks!* book. It is the teacher's questions that make the difference and incorporates the Math Standards.

STEP 1: PLAY THE GAME: ENGINE, ENGINE

Choose a group of 4 or 5 to demonstrate the game the first time you play it. After students understand the game, divide the group into equal-numbered circles.

1. Students stand in a circle. Each person holds both fists in front.

2. One person is the "conductor" who moves around the circle tapping the tops of the students' two fists in a sequence.

3. Whoever is tapped on the last word of the song is the next "conductor."

4. The "conductor" who just finished, places his or her fists behind his or her back, or plays a rhythm instrument to the beat, while the rest of the circle continues play.

5. The last student to be tapped, who has not been a "conductor," moves to a new circle of students and is the first "conductor" of the new group.

6. Begin the game again with the new circle.

TEACHER'S NOTE: Organize the small circles around the outside of the room. Establish a rotation pattern, such as each new conductor moves clockwise to the next small circle.

STEP 2: CRAFT STICK RHYTHM NOTATION

Teacher's Note: Don't tell, ask. For the CCSS Math learning process, ask questions and lead the students into thinking processes. Asking the right questions is an essential part of the learning process. Questions are the easiest way to incorporate the Common Core State Standards while teaching music. Students are more engaged in every moment of the lesson when using questions.

1. Ask the students to sit on the floor in one large circle. Lay piles of craft sticks on the floor in front of the students. Ask the students to count out six sticks.

2. **Quarter Note** (ta) "How many sticks does it take to make a 'ta'?" (1)

3. **Two Eighth Notes** (ti-ti)
"How many sticks does it take to make a 'ti-ti'?" (3)
Demonstrate and have the students make a "ti-ti."

4. **Four Sixteenth Notes** (tika-tika)
"How many sticks does it take to make a 'tika-tika'?"
Demonstrate making a ti-ti first.
Add two sticks vertically up and down inside the ti-ti.

   • Add an additional stick across the top horizontally.

5. **Quarter Rest** (shh)"How many sticks does it take to make a 'shh?'" (3)

MATH CONCEPTS IN THE MUSIC LESSON WITH CRAFT STICK PATTERNS

Now let's get started with their first composition while integrating math at the same time! Using craft sticks to create rhythm patterns provides a great opportunity to introduce algebra, counting, patterns, and other math concepts.

Rhythm patterns are full of patterns, thus the name. The following steps can be used all within one class if it is an older group, or broken down to a few steps at a time per class for a younger group.

THE FIRST CRAFT STICK 4-BEAT PATTERN

1. "How many 'things' will there be in a pattern?" (4)
    - Obviously, there are many different amounts that you could have, but to keep it simple, I start with a base of always having four things, or four counts, in a rhythm pattern. Exceptions come later.

TEACHER'S NOTE: Say "things," rather than "counts." Using the word "counts" automatically means counting and that is confusing when you're holding a bunch of sticks in your hands and talking about counting in the general classroom. It is less confusing to use the word "things," as in "four things in a rhythm pattern." (If you say how many "things" and point to a rhythm pattern in the book, they quickly can see the four different "things," which we know as counts or beats.)

2. "How can I make a "ta, ta, ti-ti, ta" rhythm pattern with sticks?" Student volunteers to come to the front and create the pattern for the class.

3. "How many sticks does it take to make the "ta, ta, ti-ti, ta" rhythm pattern?" (6)

4. Arrange the students in a circle or long lines if possible.

5. Place piles of sticks in front of groups of kids and ask them to count out six sticks and recreate the same "ta, ta, ti-ti, ta" rhythm pattern.

6. Quickly glance to assess successful task completion.

7. Ask the students to use their index finger and chant the pattern together, following along with their own pattern from left to right.

8. Repeat chanting and pointing until you ask them to stop.

TEACHER'S NOTE: Visually assess any students that need additional help, and give silent individual help by pointing with them as the class chants the rhythm pattern. This task also helps the reading skill of reading left to right, a Kindergarten CCSS ELA-Literacy Standard in the Reading: Foundational Skills strand (CCSS.ELA-LITERACY.RF.K.1.A).

9. "Make another rhythm pattern with four "things" in it using six sticks. It cannot be the same as your neighbor's pattern." Here are three examples:

10. Ask students to keep a steady beat by patting their thighs.

11. Point to the first student's pattern and have the student point to and chant it. Have the other students echo.

12. Move to the next student in line, doing the same thing, while keeping a continuous beat until finishing with the last student.

13. Add rhythm instruments.

TEACHER'S NOTE: It is essential to use the stick lessons before introducing stick mystery songs. The students now have a solid understanding of rhythm patterns.

STEP 3: INTRODUCE A MYSTERY SONG
(on a subsequent day)

Preparation: Display Chart 1 on the board.

1. "There is a mystery song on the board. If you can solve it, you get to play the game!" (Now, you need to guide them in solving the mystery.)

2. "Chant the rhythm beginning in box 1."

3. Ask the students if they see a pattern.

    *   Which two boxes are the same? (1 & 3)
    *   Which two boxes are different? (2 & 4) Why?

4. "There are special singing words that help us learn the melody."

 • Demonstrate that the first two notes are "sol's" and write an "s" under each of those notes for "sol."

 • The third and fourth notes are "mi's", so write "m's" under each of them.

5. Demonstrate singing "sol-sol, mi-mi." Students echo.

6. "What letter should you write under notes 5 & 6?" ("s's" for sol)

7. "Can you finish telling me what letters to put underneath each note?"

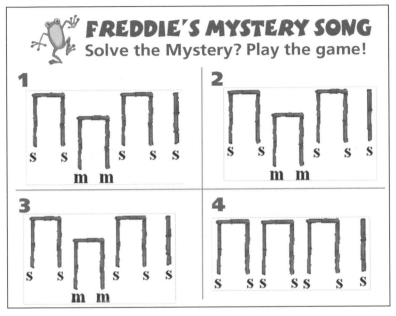

8. Echo sing each box if it is the students' first time experiencing solfege.

9. "Can anyone sing it alone?" (Without hearing it sung by you, the teacher, all the way through.)

10. Entire class sings the song in solfege without the teacher singing. Once sung successfully, ready for the last step.

11. "Does anyone recognize the singing game—the lyrics, or real words?"

12. Guide students to the answer if they need help.

13. Sing the lyrics and move to the stick activity or play the game, depending on which works best for that particular game. (For example, "Engine, Engine" works best to play the game and then get out the sticks because the students are organized in small circles at the end of the game.)

WHY RECTANGLE BOX MEASURES?

When primary students begin to read rhythm patterns, the "ta" (quarter note) is typically a single vertical line. When we draw measures of music on the board using "ta", ti-ti, and bar lines, the bar lines are confusing and the kids have difficulty knowing if it is a "ta" or a bar line.

Use rectangular boxes because they look similar to flash cards with rhythm patterns.

In addition, identifying rectangles is a Kindergarten CCSS Math Geometry Standard. (CCSS.MATH.CONTENT.K.G.A.1, CCSS.MATH.CONTENT.K.G.A.2)

Once the students are very comfortable with the rectangular boxes and how many things go in each box, then demonstrate that you can just draw the bar line instead of drawing the entire rectangular box, and it means the same thing. Because they've used boxes for so long, switching to just one line is no longer confused with a quarter note.

This saves you a lot of time and headache.

STEP 4: PLAY THE GAME

Play the "Engine, Engine" game.

STEP 5: STICKS ACTIVITY

Math and music learning abound in every stick activity. Again, lead the students into discovery learning and higher order thinking by asking leading questions rather than telling them what to do. This is a combination of music, CCSS Mathematical Practice and Mathematical Content Standards. (Standards used in the Sticks Lesson recorded on the chart below.)

ENGINE, ENGINE

1. Adjust the small circles to groups of four.

2. Students "count off" 1-4, so each student in the circle has a number in sequential order around the circle.

3. Using craft sticks, students "notate" Chart 3. *(If this is the first time, demonstrate with one group first for clarity.)*

4. "How many sticks will it take to notate box 1?" (10) Have student #1 of demonstration group notate with craft sticks on floor.

5. Continue the questioning with box 2, 3, and 4. As they answer, Students #2, #3, #4 of the demonstration group each notate their assigned box (measure) with craft sticks on the floor.

6. Also include questions, such as, "Which boxes are alike? Which are different?"

7. Once students appear to understand, place piles of sticks in the center of each circle.

8. Instruct each student to count out the number of sticks that he or she needs to notate his or her box—1, 2, 3, or 4. (10 sticks each.)

9. In each circle, Student #1 points to the first beat of his or her measure and moves finger left to right with the song; student #2 takes over on his or her measure, then #3, and finally #4.

10. Repeat the song and the process until you observe every circle successfully pointing to the rhythm and correct rhythm notation.

TEACHER'S NOTE: Repetition allows time to silently help any group while the class is actively engaged in singing and following the stick notation with their fingers. Encourage peer teaching and teamwork within groups.

◆ Record/Report the CCSS Standards Incorporated in This Lesson

Mathematical Content Standards

Notice how the CCSS change for each grade level.

Kindergarten:

CCSS.MATH.CONTENT.K.CC.A.1
Count to 100 by ones and by tens.

CCSS.MATH.CONTENT.K.CC.A.2
Count forward beginning from a given number within the known sequence (instead of having to begin at 1).

CCSS.MATH.CONTENT.K.CC.B.4
Understand the relationship between numbers and quantities; connect counting to cardinality.

CCSS.MATH.CONTENT.K.CC.B.4.A
When counting objects, say the number names in the standard order, pairing each object with one and only one number name and each number name with one and only one object.

CCSS.MATH.CONTENT.K.CC.B.4.B
Understand that the last number name said tells the number of objects counted. The number of objects is the same regardless of their arrangement or the order in which they were counted.

CCSS.MATH.CONTENT.K.CC.B.4.C
Understand that each successive number name refers to a quantity that is one larger.

CCSS.MATH.CONTENT.K.CC.B.5
Count to answer "how many?" questions about as many as 20 things arranged in a line, a rectangular array, or a circle, or as many as 10 things in a scattered configuration; given a number from 1-20, count out that many objects.

CCSS.MATH.CONTENT.K.CC.C.6

Identify whether the number of objects in one group is greater than, less than, or equal to the number of objects in another group, e.g., by using matching and counting strategies.[1]

Grade 1:

CCSS.MATH.CONTENT.1.OA.B.3

Apply properties of operations as strategies to add and subtract.2

CCSS.MATH.CONTENT.1.OA.B.4

Understand subtraction as an unknown-addend problem.

CCSS.MATH.CONTENT.1.OA.C.5

Relate counting to addition and subtraction (e.g., by counting on 2 to add 2).

Grade2: (No Grade 2 content standards in this lesson.)

Mathematical Practice Standards. Apply to Grades K-2.

CCSS.MATH.PRACTICE.MP1

Make sense of problems and persevere in solving them.

CCSS.MATH.PRACTICE.MP2

Reason abstractly and quantitatively.

CCSS.MATH.PRACTICE.MP6

Attend to precision.

CCSS.MATH.PRACTICE.MP7

Look for and make use of structure.

◆ Example: K-2 Music Lesson with CCSS That Incorporates Math and ELA/Literacy Standards

Brown Bear, Brown Bear

Bill Martin, Jr. Illustrated by by Eric Carle

Henry Holt and Co. (BYR)

I love using the storybook, *Brown Bear, Brown Bear.* The students light up when they see a familiar story from their classroom. It is an easy story to add musical elements and review/extend Common Core standards. Add a la-sol-mi melody and craft stick rhythms.

Ta   ta   ta   ta
s   m   s   m
Brown Bear, Brown Bear.

ti - ti   ta   ta-ta
s   s   l   s-m
What do you see?

ta ti-ti ta   ta
s   m m   s   m
I   see a red fox

ti- ti   ta   ta-ta
s   s   l   s-m
looking at me.

As a class, students choose new colors and animals to replace those in the storybook. Students decide if the rhythm and melody need to change or stay the same. Using craft sticks, the students notate their arrangements or measures I dictate. This type of lesson easily includes Math and ELA standards.

Depending on the lesson focus, the following CCSS may be easily included:

Kindergarten
CCSS.MATH.CONTENT.K.CC.A.2
CCSS.MATH.CONTENT.K.CC.A.4
CCSS.MATH.CONTENT.K.CC.A.5
CCSS.MATH.CONTENT.K.OA.A.1

CCSS.ELA-LITERACY.RL.K.4
CCSS.ELA-LITERACY.RL.K.6
CCSS.ELA-LITERACY.RL.K.10
CCSS.ELA-LITERACY.RF.K.1

Grade 1
CCSS.MATH.CONTENT.1.OA.A.2
CCSS.MATH.CONTENT.1.OA.C.5

CCSS.ELA-LITERACY.RL.1.10
CCSS.ELA-LITERACY.RF.1.1
CCSS.ELA-LITERACY.RF.1.2
CCSS.ELA-LITERACY.RF.1.3
CCSS.ELA-LITERACY.RF.1.4

Grade 2
CCSS.ELA-LITERACY.RF.2.3

CCSS.ELA-LITERACY.RF.2.4

◆ Example: Grades 3–5 Music Lesson with CCSS That Incorporates Math Standards

POWER UP!

The "Math Rocks" teacher's resource (Hal Leonard) includes songs already incorporating Common Core Math standards. For example the song, "Power Up!" includes counting by 5's and 7's.

Recorded Song Lyrics

REFRAIN   One, two three, four, everybody on the floor.
Five, six, seven, eight, now's the time to celebrate!
Eight, seven, six, five, everybody look alive.
Four, three, two, one, power-up and have some fun!

RAP 1   5, 10, 15, 20, 25, 30, 35, 40, 45, 50, 55, 60, 65, 70, 75, GO!!

(repeat Refrain)

RAP 2   7, 14, 21, 28, 35, 42, 49, 56, 63, 70, 77, 84, 91, 98, 105!!

(repeat Refrain)

How to Incorporate Common Core Math (Grade 3)

1. Have students practice counting by 7's before singing the song again.

2. A lesson worksheet asks students to write the answers for counting by 5's and 7's, and then count by a new number assigned by the teacher. Ask the classroom teacher which multiplication facts need review or what they are currently working on in the classroom, and use that information to assign new numbers.

3. Make record of the collaboration with the classroom teacher and the Math Content and Practice standards incorporated. (Included in the Math Rocks resource for easy reference.) Below is a sample of the lesson worksheet that corresponds to the song, "Power up!"

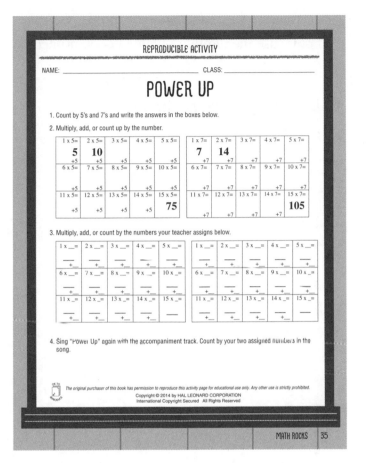

REPRODUCIBLE ACTIVITY

NAME: _____ CLASS: _____

POWER UP

1. Count by 5's and 7's and write the answers in the boxes below.

2. Multiply, add, or count up by the number.

1 x 5=	2 x 5=	3 x 5=	4 x 5=	5 x 5=
5	**10**			
+5	+5	+5	+5	+5
6 x 5=	7 x 5=	8 x 5=	9 x 5=	10 x 5=
+5	+5	+5	+5	+5
11 x 5=	12 x 5=	13 x 5=	14 x 5=	15 x 5=
+5	+5	+5	+5	**75**

1 x 7=	2 x 7=	3 x 7=	4 x 7=	5 x 7=
7	**14**			
+7	+7	+7	+7	+7
6 x 7=	7 x 7=	8 x 7=	9 x 7=	10 x 7=
+7	+7	+7	+7	+7
11 x 7=	12 x 7=	13 x 7=	14 x 7=	15 x 7=
+7	+7	+7	+7	**105**

3. Multiply, add, or count by the numbers your teacher assigns below.

1 x __=	2 x __=	3 x __=	4 x __=	5 x __=
+__	+__	+__	+__	+__
6 x __=	7 x __=	8 x __=	9 x __=	10 x __=
+__	+__	+__	+__	+__
11 x __=	12 x __=	13 x __=	14 x __=	15 x __=
+__	+__	+__	+__	____

1 x __=	2 x __=	3 x __=	4 x __=	5 x __=
+__	+__	+__	+__	+__
6 x __=	7 x __=	8 x __=	9 x __=	10 x __=
+__	+__	+__	+__	+__
11 x __=	12 x __=	13 x __=	14 x __=	15 x __=
+__	+__	+__	+__	

4. Sing "Power Up" again with the accompaniment track. Count by your two assigned numbers in the song.

MATH ROCKS | 35

4. Sing Power Up! again with the accompaniment track. Count by your two assigned numbers in the song.

CCSS Standard Incorporated in This Lesson
GRADE 3: CCSS.MATH.CONTENT.3.OA.C.7 Multiply and divide within 100.

Want more lesson ideas?

◆ Additional Help

The Common Core in K-5 Music Online Course includes a Lesson Swap. Music teachers taking the course share lesson ideas incorporating Common Core State Standards. Students of the course have full access to the Lesson Swap, giving credit to the creators, of course. http://www.CommonCoreinK5Music.com

NOTE: To access digital files of the charts and templates in Appendixes A, B & C, use the digital download code printed on the first page.

◆ Appendix A: CCSS Mathematics Charts

Grades K-2 Math Overview

Grades K-2 CCSS MATH Overview
See Grade Level CCSS MATH Standards for specific codes.
Include Mathematical Practices in each grade. (Listed below chart.)
Focus instructional time on listed critical areas per grade.

Kindergarten
CCSS MATH Content Standards
More detailed explanations located at:
http://www.corestandards.org/Math/Content/K/introduction

Critical Focus Areas
1. Representing and comparing whole numbers, initially with sets of objects
2. Describing shapes and space

More learning time in Kindergarten should be devoted to number than to other topics.

Grade 1
CCSS MATH Content Standards
More detailed explanations located at:
http://www.corestandards.org/Math/Content/1/introduction

Critical Focus Areas
1. Developing understanding of
   • Addition
   • Subtraction
   • Strategies for addition and subtraction within 20
2. Developing understanding of
   • Whole number relationships and place value
   • Including grouping in tens and ones
3. Developing understanding of
   • Linear measurement
   • Measuring lengths as iterating length units
4. Reasoning about attributes of, and composing and decomposing geometric shapes

Grade 2
CCSS MATH Content Standards
More detailed explanations located at:
http://www.corestandards.org/Math/Content/2/introduction

Critical Focus Areas
1. Extending understanding of base-ten notation
2. Building fluency with addition and subtraction
3. Using standard units of measure
4. Describing and analyzing shapes

Chart Organization by Sharon Burch
Copyright © 2015 by HAL LEONARD CORPORATION
Complete Common Core State Standards, additional information and footnotes at http://www.CoreStandards.org
© Copyright 2010. National Governors Association Center for Best Practices and Council of Chief State School Officers.
1

Grades K-2 CCSS MATH Overview

Kindergarten CCSS MATH Content Standards More detailed explanations located at: http://www.corestandards.org/Math/Content/K/introduction	Grade 1 CCSS MATH Content Standards More detailed explanations located at: http://www.corestandards.org/Math/Content/1/introduction	Grade 2 CCSS MATH Content Standards More detailed explanations located at: http://www.corestandards.org/Math/Content/2/introduction
Domains **CC. Counting and Cardinality** A. Know number names and the count sequence. B. Count to tell the number of objects. C. Compare numbers. **OA. Operations and Algebraic Thinking** A. Understand addition as putting together and adding to, and understand subtraction as taking apart and taking from. **NBT. Number and Operations in Base Ten** A. Work with numbers 11-19 to gain foundations for place value. **MD. Measurement and Data** A. Describe and compare measurable attributes. B. Classify objects and count the number of objects in each category **G. Geometry** A. Identify and describe shapes. B. Analyze, compare, create, and compose shapes.	**Domains** **OA. Operations and Algebraic Thinking** A. Represent and solve problems involving addition and subtraction. B. Understand and apply properties of operations and the relationship between addition and subtraction. C. Add and subtract within 20. D. Work with addition and subtraction equations. **NBT. Number and Operations in Base Ten** A. Extend the counting sequence. B. Understand place value. C. Use place value understanding and properties of operations to add and subtract. **MD. Measurement and Data** A. Measure lengths indirectly and by iterating length units. B. Tell and write time. C. Represent and interpret data. **G. Geometry** A. Reason with shapes and their attributes.	**Domains** **OA. Operations and Algebraic Thinking** A. Represent and solve problems involving addition and subtraction. B. Add and subtract within 20. C. Work with equal groups of objects to gain foundations for multiplication. **NBT. Number and Operations in Base Ten** A. Understand place value. B. Use place value understanding and properties of operations to add and subtract. **MD. Measurement and Data** A. Measure and estimate lengths in standard units. B. Relate addition and subtraction to length. C. Work with time and money. D. Represent and interpret data. **G. Geometry** A. Reason with shapes and their attributes.

Mathematical Practices Apply to all grade levels

CCSS.MATH.PRACTICE.MP1 Make sense of problems and persevere in solving them.
CCSS.MATH.PRACTICE.MP2 Reason abstractly and quantitatively.
CCSS.MATH.PRACTICE.MP3 Construct viable arguments and critique the reasoning of others.
CCSS.MATH.PRACTICE.MP4 Model with mathematics.
CCSS.MATH.PRACTICE.MP5 Use appropriate tools strategically.
CCSS.MATH.PRACTICE.MP6 Attend to precision.
CCSS.MATH.PRACTICE.MP7 Look for and make use of structure.
CCSS.MATH.PRACTICE.MP8 Look for and express regularity in repeated reasoning.

Grades 3-5 Math Overview
(located in the digital download)

◆ Appendix B: CCSS English Language Arts/Literacy Charts

CCR - English Language Arts/Literacy College and Career Readiness Anchor Standards

English Language Arts College and Career Readiness Anchor Standards – K-12 Broad Standards
http://www.CoreStandards.org/ELA-Literacy/CCRA/R/

READING	WRITING	SPEAKING & LISTENING	LANGUAGE
Key Ideas and Details	**Text Types and Purposes[1]**	**Comprehension and Collaboration**	**Conventions of Standard English**
CCSS.ELA-LITERACY.CCRA.R.1 Read closely to determine what the text says explicitly and to make logical inferences from it; cite specific textual evidence when writing or speaking to support conclusions drawn from the text.	**CCSS.ELA-LITERACY.CCRA.W.1** Write arguments to support claims in an analysis of substantive topics or texts using valid reasoning and relevant and sufficient evidence.	**CCSS.ELA-LITERACY.CCRA.SL.1** Prepare for and participate effectively in a range of conversations and collaborations with diverse partners, building on others' ideas and expressing their own clearly and persuasively.	**CCSS.ELA-LITERACY.CCRA.L.1** Demonstrate command of the conventions of standard English grammar and usage when writing or speaking.
CCSS.ELA-LITERACY.CCRA.R.2 Determine central ideas or themes of a text and analyze their development; summarize the key supporting details and ideas.	**CCSS.ELA-LITERACY.CCRA.W.2** Write informative/explanatory texts to examine and convey complex ideas and information clearly and accurately through the effective selection, organization, and analysis of content.	**CCSS.ELA-LITERACY.CCRA.SL.2** Integrate and evaluate information presented in diverse media and formats, including visually, quantitatively, and orally.	**CCSS.ELA-LITERACY.CCRA.L.2** Demonstrate command of the conventions of standard English capitalization, punctuation, and spelling when writing.
CCSS.ELA-LITERACY.CCRA.R.3 Analyze how and why individuals, events, or ideas develop and interact over the course of a text.	**CCSS.ELA-LITERACY.CCRA.W.3** Write narratives to develop real or imagined experiences or events using effective technique, well-chosen details and well-structured event sequences.	**CCSS.ELA-LITERACY.CCRA.SL.3** Evaluate a speaker's point of view, reasoning, and use of evidence and rhetoric.	**Knowledge of Language**
Craft and Structure	**Production and Distribution of Writing**	**Presentation of Knowledge and Ideas**	**CCSS.ELA-LITERACY.CCRA.L.3** Apply knowledge of language to understand how language functions in different contexts, to make effective choices for meaning or style, and to comprehend more fully when reading or listening.
CCSS.ELA-LITERACY.CCRA.R.4 Interpret words and phrases as they are used in a text, including determining technical, connotative, and figurative meanings, and analyze how specific word choices shape meaning or tone.	**CCSS.ELA-LITERACY.CCRA.W.4** Produce clear and coherent writing in which the development, organization, and style are appropriate to task, purpose, and audience.	**CCSS.ELA-LITERACY.CCRA.SL.4** Present information, findings, and supporting evidence such that listeners can follow the line of reasoning and the organization, development, and style are appropriate to task, purpose, and audience.	**Vocabulary Acquisition and Use**
CCSS.ELA-LITERACY.CCRA.R.5 Analyze the structure of texts, including how specific sentences, paragraphs, and larger portions of the text (e.g., a section, chapter, scene, or stanza) relate to each other and the whole.	**CCSS.ELA-LITERACY.CCRA.W.5** Develop and strengthen writing as needed by planning, revising, editing, rewriting, or trying a new approach.	**CCSS.ELA-LITERACY.CCRA.SL.5** Make strategic use of digital media and visual displays of data to express information and enhance understanding of presentations.	**CCSS.ELA-LITERACY.CCRA.L.4** Determine or clarify the meaning of unknown and multiple-meaning words and phrases by using context clues, analyzing meaningful word parts, and consulting general and specialized reference materials, as appropriate.
CCSS.ELA-LITERACY.CCRA.R.6 Assess how point of view or purpose shapes the content and style of a text.	**CCSS.ELA-LITERACY.CCRA.W.6** Use technology, including the Internet, to produce and publish writing and to interact and collaborate with others.	**CCSS.ELA-LITERACY.CCRA.SL.6** Adapt speech to a variety of contexts and communicative tasks, demonstrating command of formal English when indicated or appropriate.	**CCSS.ELA-LITERACY.CCRA.L.5** Demonstrate understanding of figurative language, word relationships, and nuances in word meanings.

Chart Organization by Sharon Burch
Copyright © 2015 by HAL LEONARD CORPORATION
Complete Common Core State Standards, additional information and footnotes at http://www.CoreStandards.org
© Copyright 2010. National Governors Association Center for Best Practices and Council of Chief State School Officers.

1

Grades K ELA-Literacy: Writing, Speaking & Listening, Language

Kindergarten CCSS ELA-Literacy: Writing, Speaking & Listening, and Language Strands
Standards and Additional Information located at www.CoreStandards.org

W Writing¹	SL Speaking & Listening	L Language
Text Types and Purposes	**Comprehension and Collaboration**	**Conventions of Standard English**
CCSS.ELA-LITERACY.W.K.1 Use a combination of drawing, dictating, and writing to compose opinion pieces in which they tell a reader the topic or the name of the book they are writing about and state an opinion or preference about the topic or book (e.g., *My favorite book is...*).	CCSS.ELA-LITERACY.SL.K.1 Participate in collaborative conversations with diverse partners about *kindergarten topics and texts* with peers and adults in small and larger groups.	CCSS.ELA-LITERACY.L.K.1 Demonstrate command of the conventions of standard English grammar and usage when writing or speaking.
CCSS.ELA-LITERACY.W.K.2 Use a combination of drawing, dictating, and writing to compose informative/explanatory texts in which they name what they are writing about and supply some information about the topic.	• CCSS.ELA-LITERACY.SL.K.1.A Follow agreed-upon rules for discussions (e.g., listening to others and taking turns speaking about the topics and texts under discussion).	• CCSS.ELA-LITERACY.L.K.1.A Print many upper- and lowercase letters.
	• CCSS.ELA-LITERACY.SL.K.1.B Continue a conversation through multiple exchanges.	• CCSS.ELA-LITERACY.L.K.1.B Use frequently occurring nouns and verbs.
CCSS.ELA-LITERACY.W.K.3 Use a combination of drawing, dictating, and writing to narrate a single event or several loosely linked events, tell about the events in the order in which they occurred, and provide a reaction to what happened.	CCSS.ELA-LITERACY.SL.K.2 Confirm understanding of a text read aloud or information presented orally or through other media by asking and answering questions about key details and requesting clarification if something is not understood.	• CCSS.ELA-LITERACY.L.K.1.C Form regular plural nouns orally by adding /s/ or /es/ (e.g., *dog, dogs; wish, wishes*).
Production and Distribution of Writing (W.K.4 begins in grade 3)	CCSS.ELA-LITERACY.SL.K.3 Ask and answer questions in order to seek help, get information, or clarify something that is not understood.	• CCSS.ELA-LITERACY.L.K.1.D Understand and use question words (interrogatives) (e.g., *who, what, where, when, why, how*).
CCSS.ELA-LITERACY.W.K.5 With guidance and support from adults, respond to questions and suggestions from peers and add details to strengthen writing as needed.	**Presentation of Knowledge and Ideas**	• CCSS.ELA-LITERACY.L.K.1.E Use the most frequently occurring prepositions (e.g., *to, from, in, out, on, off, for, of, by with*).
CCSS.ELA-LITERACY.W.K.6 With guidance and support from adults, explore a variety of digital tools to produce and publish writing, including in collaboration with peers.	CCSS.ELA-LITERACY.SL.K.4 Describe familiar people, places, things, and events and, with prompting and support, provide additional detail.	• CCSS.ELA-LITERACY.L.K.1.F Produce and expand complete sentences in shared language activities.
	CCSS.ELA-LITERACY.SL.K.5 Add drawings or other visual displays to descriptions as desired to provide additional detail.	CCSS.ELA-LITERACY.L.K.2 Demonstrate command of the conventions of standard English capitalization, punctuation, and spelling when writing.
	CCSS.ELA-LITERACY.SL.K.6 Speak audibly and express thoughts, feelings, and ideas clearly.	• CCSS.ELA-LITERACY.L.K.2.A Capitalize the first word in a sentence and the pronoun.
		• CCSS.ELA-LITERACY.L.K.2.B Recognize and name end punctuation.

Chart Organization by Sharon Burch
Copyright © 2015 by HAL LEONARD CORPORATION
Complete Common Core State Standards, additional information and footnotes at http://www.CoreStandards.org
© Copyright 2010. National Governors Association Center for Best Practices and Council of Chief State School Officers.

1

Grades K-5 ELA-Literacy Charts
(located in the digital download)

◆ Appendix C: Lesson Plan Templates

Lesson Plan with Music and CCSS Chart Template

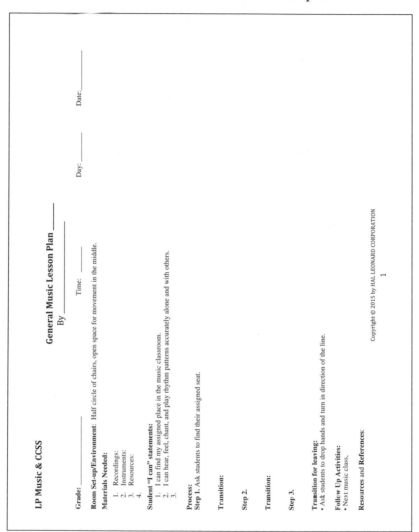

LP Music & CCSS

General Music Lesson Plan ___

By ___

Grade: ___   Time: ___   Day: ___   Date: ___

Room Set-up/Environment: Half circle of chairs, open space for movement in the middle.

Materials Needed:
1. Recordings:
2. Instruments:
3. Resources:
4.

Student "I can" statements:
1. I can find my assigned place in the music classroom.
2. I can hear, feel, chant, and play rhythm patterns accurately alone and with others.
3.

Process:
Step 1. Ask students to find their assigned seat.

Transition:

Step 2.

Transition:

Step 3.

Transition for leaving:
• Ask students to drop hands and turn in direction of the line.

Follow Up Activities:
• Next music class,

Resources and References:

Copyright © 2015 by HAL LEONARD CORPORATION

1

LP Music & CCSS

General Music Lesson Plan ___

By ___

Music Standards Incorporated in this MUSIC LESSON:

CCSS Standards Incorporated in this MUSIC LESSON:

GRADE ___ CCSS.ELA-LITERACY STANDARDS

GRADE ___ CCSS.MATH.CONTENT STANDARDS

	CCSS.MATH.PRACTICE STANDARDS							
	MP1	MP2	MP3	MP4	MP5	MP6	MP7	MP8

CCSS codes located at www.CoreStandards.org.

Copyright © 2015 by HAL LEONARD CORPORATION

2

Lesson Plan & Documentation Charts
(located in the digital download)

◆ Appendix D: Suggested Resources to Incorporate CCSS

GRADES PreK-K

Brown Bear, Brown Bear
Bill Martin Jr; Illustrated by Eric Carle
Henry Holt and Co. (BYR)
Holt Books for Young Readers
Henry Holt and Co. (BYR)
April 1992
Hardcover
ISBN: 9780805017441
ISBN10: 0805017445
Picture Book
8.38 x 10.23 inches, 28 pages
Full-color illustrations throughout
Age Range: 2 to 5
Grade Range: P to K

GRADES K-3

Sticks! by Sharon Burch (Shawnee Press/Hal Leonard)

AlphaBOP by John Jacobson (Hal Leonard)

NumberBOP by John Jacobson (Hal Leonard)

GRADES 2-5

Sound Stories by Cristi Cary Miller (Hal Leonard)

Sound Poems by Cristi Cary Miller (Hal Leonard)

GRADES 3-5

Math Rocks! by Roger Emerson/John Jacobson (Hal Leonard)

Grammar Rocks! by Roger Emerson/John Jacobson
(Hal Leonard)